Life Is a Pop Quiz

Are You Passing the Test?

David Scrimshaw

Life is a Pop Quiz
Are You Passing the Test?
by David Scrimshaw

Printed in the United States of America

ISBN 9781619968080

Unless otherwise indicated, Bible quotations are taken from The New King James Version of the Bible.

www.xulonpress.com

To my Mother and Father

Table of Contents

Foreword

There are many different reasons that a teacher would administer a pop quiz. Having been both a college instructor and a secondary school teacher, I can say that not all pop quizzes have a rational basis.

It seems to me that many a quiz has appeared in students' lives as an attempt to revive the student's grades – a sort of CPR for the student who forgot to "feed, water, exercise and train" his academic life. In such cases, the quiz acts to test or assess knowledge the student *should have had* before taking the subject he or she is allowing to wither. Such quizzes do nothing to help the student's mastery of the material being ***ignored*** and consequently the education vine shrivels and dies. Such "tests" are designed to make the student feel better about himself or obtain a passing grade when one has not been earned. This may be attributed to administrative/parental pressure placed on the teacher, who does not wish to lose his or her position.

But there ***are*** good pop quizzes. A science lab or language lab often has pop quizzes. They are designed to combine both hands-on or tongue-on practical experience with conceptual "book-learning," which makes a deeper impact on the student's mind, thus providing more long-lasting results. More importantly, these quizzes tend to give a more realistic "snapshot" of how well the student *actually* understands the material. These quizzes give an accurate report to the teacher. After all, teachers can neither read minds nor hearts. Even more significantly, such quizzes demonstrate to the student how he or she is doing in the subject being assessed.

But the topic of this book is *life* being like a pop quiz. Actually, life is the course and each day is filled with quizzes of the pop variety. All of us have had varying degrees of success with these quizzes. But if the truth be told, many of them result in very low scores.

It is my hope that as a result of your reading this book and meditating on the precepts found therein, you will find an improvement in your overall "score" in life. And at its end, you will find not only *eternal* credit for the course, but a *prize* as well.

1

The Best Teacher
Is Found in the Correct Manual

I n college, I remember being assigned what seemed an arbitrary time of day to sign up for my first freshman classes. There were those who had lucked out and were among the first to get the "good professors" and then there were the rest of us who had to take first year instructors or classes that clashed with extra-curricular opportunities such as drama, debate, fraternities, and service or paying jobs. As it turned out, some of these instructors we were warned about turned out to be challenging as well as interesting; an example of a life pop quiz.

But Who is the teacher of life? You need a manual or text book to answer that one. Let me ask you, who made the car you drive? Was it Ford, or Toyota, or Subaru? If you want to know something about your Ford, do you read the car manual written by and for Subarus? No, you want to read the correct manual.

So it is with life. You need to read the manual of the One Who made life. All forms of life, and just for good measure, Who made the universe as well. Now I know you are going to say that there are a lot of manuals out there. I know of people who have spent a lifetime reading manuals, and all they have to show for it is confusion.

Pop Quiz #1 – How do you tell which manual is the right one?

Life Lab – *Secret Service Counterfeit Training*

When the Secret Service instructs their agents in detecting false or phony "funny money," they do not have them study every known counterfeiter in the history of mankind. That would take decades, if not longer. Some of you might suggest that they stick to studying only counterfeit American bills. Others might consider only bills faked in the last thirty or forty years.

But that is not what they do. They study **only** the **real** product. They touch it, examine it under microscopes, learn about the red and blue cloth made into the paper, examine the engraving, etc. They become experts on that which is **real.**

From the Teacher –

Let me point out to you the **real owner's manual** – written by the One Who owns all. If I were to give you the modern rendering of this manual's title, it would be "The Separated Book," otherwise known as "**The Holy**, which means separated, **Bible**, or book." Separated from what? Other books. Other views. Other philosophies. Other opinions. This world is no different than the world of the Secret Service. There is that which is real, hence valuable and then there is the false, the sham and the lie, which is worthless.

If you were to study these other books, you would find things that appear to be good.

Many of these writings have a variation of the golden rule, "And as ye would that men should do to you, do ye also to them likewise" (Luke 6:31). While reading these various books, one could become confused, just as the Secret Service agents who might study both real and false currencies at the same time. The lines between false and real tend to merge.

So my suggestion is: study what is real. What makes the Bible the **real** manual? Notice that the Bible, written by many different humans over a period of more than one thousand years, maintains a tone and theme from beginning to end. How did this happen? It happened because the Great Teacher is also the Creator and the Bible's Author.

Answer to Pop Quiz #1 – The book which provides the answer for a person's need to be forgiven of his or her sins is the **real** manual.

Homework Assignment

Read the following interesting facts and Scripture references:

1) There is only One Creator God, Who has many titles and a single revealed name – "I AM" (see Exodus 3:14).

2) This Creator/Teacher has one standard: perfection (think: 100%, A+).

3) He does not want His students to fail the course because He loves them (think: 99% or lower, less than perfect, failure means 'H' as in Hell).

4) The problem is that ever since His first class (think: Garden of Eden, co-students Adam and Eve,) where His students earned and possessed the "failing gene," has passed on that gene

of failure to all their children (think: Us).

5) The Great Teacher or Creator promised His first co-student, Eve, that she would produce an heir Who would defeat this failing-gene problem (see Genesis 3:15).

6) The remainder of these separate books within what is known as the Old Testament of "The Separated Book" forecast the failings of the "class of Beginnings" or mankind. They also tell what the One Who is coming to change our future will be like so that we can know Him and be changed by Him (see Isaiah 7:14, 9:6-7, 35:4-6, 53:1-12, Psalm 22).

2

How Do I Stop Failing
And Start Passing?

At one time in my teaching career, I taught in a Christian school where my three children were enrolled. My oldest son was in one of my classes. Normally, you don't want to instruct your own child due to "conflict of interests" accusations. This was not a large school, and I taught three levels of Science and two levels of Spanish – there was really no one else available to teach him.

Consider the Creator's position: He spends time with His students every day (Genesis 3:8). The Bible was being written for Adam and Eve, so to speak, and the only rule for them was not to eat the fruit of a certain tree (Genesis 2:17). Classes had barely begun when the bell rang. Sin, which is failing on a permanent level, now existed in the entire student body! Adam, by the way, is listed as God's created son (Luke 3:38).

Did that mean that class was out for good? No.

Pop Quiz #2 – Who is the Savior?

Given: We have the right manual or textbook.

Given: We know the Creator has sent One Who will change our failing gene. He is known as the Wonderful Counselor, Prince of Peace, and Messiah (Anointed One).

Given: Jesus of Nazareth fulfills every forecast (prophecy) regarding the One Who would save us from our failing (sinful) status. Read the books called the gospels, or the good news, according to Matthew (a tax collector), Mark (a student of Peter), Luke (a doctor), and John (a student of Jesus).

Find: The Savior.

Life Lab – *Read Mark 2:1-12.*

There are times when we need friends to help us. So it was with the man in this passage. Something had gone wrong in his life many years ago. He knew he had wronged the Creator. He could no longer move as a result. His friends had heard of One Who made the blind to see and the lame to walk. After searching for the One Who could help their friend, they found Jesus, the One, teaching in someone's home.

Due to the crowd, there was only one way they could get their friend to see Him – tear open a hole in the roof and lower their friend down to the Prince of Peace. When Jesus saw their **faith** (a prerequisite in the course of life), He took care of this man's most pressing need: He **forgave** the man's sins (verse 5.)

Then, to **demonstrate** that Jesus had, and even to this day still has, the **authority** to forgive sins, He told the man to **rise,** something he could not do before meeting Jesus, **pick up your bed,** also previously impossible for the man to accomplish, and **go home.** And all who saw it glorified the Creator, God.

From the Teacher –

Your need may not be for healing. However, your need is just as great as was the need of this man. Every human being ever born has needed this one thing to have eternal life: a **way** to be forgiven. It is impossible to "un-break a vase" once it has been broken. You cannot "un-ring a bell" once it has sounded forth. In the same manner, once you have sinned, you yourself cannot repair the damage done. You need someone else to do it. And since the Creator requires satisfaction for the injury of our sin, which is called atonement (Romans 5:11), a perfect sacrifice is demanded (2 Corinthians 5:21, 1 Peter 2:21-22).

Answer to Pop Quiz #2 – Read John 3:16-21.

Homework Assignment

Read the following questions and Scripture references:

If you have not come to the place in your course of life where you know Jesus as your Savior, answer the following questions. There are references to guide you.

1) Do you realize that you are not per-fect, that you have sinned against the Creator God? (see Romans 3:23)

   _____

2) Do you realize that if you remain imper-fect in sin until the day you die, on that day you will enter into a place that was not prepared for you (hell) because you would not receive God's free gift of forgiveness He offers through His

Son, Jesus the Anointed One (Christ)?
(Romans 6:23) _____

_____

_____

3) Do you accept as true for yourself that
God showed His love for us by having
His Son die for our sins even while
we were in rebellion against Him?
(Romans 5:8) _____

_____

4) Will you now confess verbally (out
loud) your trust in Jesus to save you
and believe (have faith in) that God
the Father raised Jesus from the dead?
(Romans 10:9) _____ If so, you are
now saved.

5) **Assurance** – "Whosoever (that means
you) shall call upon the name of the
Lord shall be saved." (Romans 10:13)

If you have done this, write your name here, just as it appears in the Lamb's (another name for Jesus) Book of Life in Heaven _____

3

Pop Quizzes for the Eternally Alive
The Poor in Spirit

You may recall that I mentioned that pop quizzes in school have varying degrees of usefulness or quality. The quizzes of life are of a whole other nature. The tests that come to us prior to having Christ as one's Savior are designed to demonstrate to us one thing: that apart from God we are failures (Galatians 3:24-26). We have failed our Creator as a servant, as a friend, and as a member of Creation itself (Romans 8:20-22). Creation is waiting for the day that we receive eternal credit for the course of life from the One Who made it all.

If you have written your name in the blank as the answer to question five in the homework for Chapter Two, the quizzes now have a different design. You are no longer in the class of those who are failing. You are now in the "class (kingdom) of the transformed." The Creator has been gracious to you and has showed His mercy toward you. He has given you the faith you needed to believe on His only begotten Son (Ephesians 2:8) and has begun the process of making you like Him (I Corinthians 15:49, 2 Corinthians 5:17).

Pop Quiz #3 – What does a "new creation" look like?

Life Lab – *Read Matthew 5:3 – The Poor in Spirit*

Since we need to grow in a new direction, the Creator left instructions for us as to what direction we should take. In science labs where one grows a culture, there are always illustrations of how the objects growing in the Petri dish should appear. Depending on what one is trying to grow, the "food" in the dish can be altered by changing pH factors, light and other variables. When the experiment turns out the way the Creator designed, there is happiness (blessedness).

Step 1 – Place the dish (you) in the light (study the Bible, pray, serve Him and others).

Step 2 – Clean the dish (you) of all that promotes the growth of pride.

Step 3 – Seek true humility and test the dish (you) often for traces of pride.

Find – Happiness (blessedness), a by-product of pleasing the Creator.

From the Teacher –

Those who have just entered this new kingdom class of heaven were made by the Creator to realize that they needed a change. In other words, they recognized the poor condition of their spirits.

Here are some words to study:

1) **poor** (*ptochos*) – cringing, abject poverty

2) **in spirit** – meaning one's spiritual condition

The student in the kingdom class realizes that he or she is utterly destitute of any understanding of the Creator apart from that which He gives in His mercy. The student's Petri dish is empty and he is completely dependent on the Creator for spiritual nourishment.

Humility is produced by the Creator, and those in His kingdom class are required to practice it.

Answer to Pop Quiz #3 – A humble and broken personality that sees he or she is a beggar before God.

Homework Assignment

1) Read the following passages and match the meanings:

    A. humble and   1) _____ Psalm
        contrite of spirit   51:17

    B. brokenhearted,   2) _____ Isaiah
        crushed in spirit   66:2

    C. contrite heart   3) _____ Psalm
                     34:18

2) Read Luke 18:9-14.

Which person shows a proud spirit?

_____

Which person shows a humble spirit?

_____

One of these individuals went home "justified," which means the Creator accepted his words of repentance and brought him into His kingdom.

Which one was "justified"? _____

What is the desired substance in the Petri dish? _____

What is the desired outcome of the experiment? _____

Answers are found at the end of book.

4

Nothing Leads to Something
Those Who Mourn

I f you have successfully completed the lab for Chapter Three, you learned that, spiritually speaking, we know that nothing good lives in human flesh (Romans 7:18.) The result is we sense our own smallness or develop humility.

According to Aristotle, nature abhors a vacuum. Therefore, a sense of smallness or humility is like causing a vacuum in our soul.

This leads to an awareness that something else should take place within us.

Pop Quiz #4 – If there is sin in a believer's life, will there be mourning?

Life Lab – *Read Matthew 5:4 – Demonstrating the Incompatibility of Sin*

This experiment, when conducted properly, also produces happiness as a by-product. For this experiment a model believer, Job, will be required. It will also be necessary to produce a vacuum in his life by taking away everything dear to him.

Step 1 – Establish the **believer status of Job:** "was perfect (complete) and upright, and one that feared God (the Creator), and eschewed (turned from) evil" (Job 1:1).

Step 2 – How to discover the incompatibility or sin:

a) Place a godly person, who has not suffered loss, before his Creator (Job 1).

b) Take away things/people he holds dear (Job 2).

c) Observe reaction(s): Job justifies himself – says he doesn't deserve the vacuum or loss he's suffered (Job 3, 6, 9:2).

d) The Creator displays His sovereignty, wisdom and holiness (Job 38).

e) Result: The believer discovers the deep sinful nature in himself, even though he has been "good" (Job 42:6).

This procedure precipitates mourning over one's sins.

From the Teacher –

Caution – It should be noted that mourning over sins is a rare occurrence today, as evidenced by the removal of mourners' benches from churches and the lack of godliness among believers (2 Timothy 4:3-4).

A word study may be helpful in understanding the precipitate which should form.

1) **Mourn** (*pentheo*) – the deepest form of grief, as in loss of a loved-one

2) **Comforted** (*parakaleo*) – to sit beside, counsel, comfort, which the Creator does for His children on a regular basis

Answer to Pop Quiz #4 – There will be deep sadness over offending the Creator.

Homework Assignment

You are to determine if real mourning has precipitated:

1) Does the believer have concern over what his/her sins have done to the Creator's reputation (due to the believer's relationship with Him)?
   Circle answer: (yes)   (no)
2) Does the believer have concern over the sins of fellow believers (read Daniel 9:5)? Circle answer: (yes)   (no)
3) As a result of mourning, has the believer experienced the Creator's forgiveness and the resulting sense of comfort? Circle: (yes)   (no)

If all answers are in the affirmative, real mourning has taken place. If any answers are negative, a greater sensitivity needs to be developed.

When this heightened awareness is achieved, *humility* (sense of nothingness) has precipitated *mourning* (sense of loss from one's sins) yielding *comfort* (of forgiveness from the Creator).

5

Producing a
Non-reactive Substance
The Meek

This lab involves the production of meekness by the Creator in the life of a transformed person. Meekness is a rarely occurring substance. It must be created under controlled conditions by the Creator's Spirit. When produced, it eradicates all other contaminants which are undesired or highly unstable. In order to understand how happiness becomes a by-product, the nature of meekness must be clearly defined.

Pop Quiz # 5 – How does meekness differ from weakness or vigilantism?

Life Lab – *Read Matthew 5:5 – The Meek*

The purpose of this lab is two-fold:

1) the removal of harmful substances
2) the simultaneous production of a desirable substance as a replacement.

At times, certain substances are defined by what they are **not**. So it is with meekness, the desirable substance, which is **not** one of the following contaminants, or undesirable substances:

- Weakness
- Cowardice
- Niceness (often confused with kind-ness, which is desirable)

Meekness, in terms of polarity, is the opposite of violence and vigilantism. Both of the above are highly unstable, reactive and dangerous substances which must be avoided at all times by the believer.

In order to fully understand the process, a brief word study of the term is necessary:

meek (*praos*) – gentle, mild, submissive, tender as in strength under control.

Warning – This lab is a difficult one to perform. It is **not** impossible. Strict self-control is to be exercised in every phase of this lab.

This lab is to be conducted by observation or reading the life lab of Joseph which begins in Genesis 37 and continues through to Genesis 45.

From the Teacher –

Meekness, or power under the control of the Creator's Spirit, yields an **inheritance**.

It is amazing that meekness, a substance which the "failing class" of mankind regards as worthless, should result in **inheriting** (*kleronomeo*) – receiving one's portion, of the earth—which is a happy by-product.

Note – Meekness is a command from the Creator (Zephaniah 2:3.) It gives the Creator the glory due Him and demonstrates patient, waiting obedience to Him on the part of the child of God.

Answer to Pop Quiz # 5 – Meekness is quiet strength which seeks the Creator's will to be done, not its own.

Homework Assignment

1) Read Genesis 37:27-28. Now read Genesis 45:1-15. Joseph was betrayed by his family. Years later, he is the second most powerful man in the world.

   What was Joseph's sign of meekness?

   _____

   _____

   _____

   _____

   _____

2) Read Matthew 26:53. Jesus is being arrested yet has committed no wrong. What does He reveal as the strength He would **not** use? _____

   _____

_____

_____

_____

Answers are at the end of the book.

6

Producing a Positive Vacuum
Those Who Hunger and Thirst for Righteousness

I n the physical world, a vacuum is thought of as a space containing no gases, or air, which creates a negative pressure outside itself. In Lab Four, we saw how a sense of mourning is produced, utilizing one kind of vacuum.

The vacuum in this lab, however, is one described as a hunger and thirst for a spiritual quality: **righteousness**. Since this vacuum is not a naturally occurring one in the "failing human class," it has as its creative source the Spirit of God. In order for the "failing class" to have some insight into what this vacuum is like, the terms *hunger* and *thirst* are used, which are terms all human beings can readily identify as an empty space in one's stomach and a parched mouth and throat.

We know we have a need for food and drink. One who is starving thinks only of the need to eat food. In this lab, food and drink are replaced by the term righteousness, which is necessary for spiritual or eternal life.

Pop Quiz #6 – What is the fuel for the soul of the Creator's child?

Life Lab – *Read Matthew 5:6 – The Hungry and Thirsty*

Note — This lab differs from the first three labs in that this lab has fulfillment as its end result.

When one places a lighted candle on a flat plate and then places over it an inverted glass tumbler, one may observe the shrinking of the flame and its extinguishment. Two things happened. Air, the fuel source of the flame, was used up or depleted and the flame went out. Secondly, a vacuum was created.

Spiritually, the candle represents the believer who was starved of the air it **must** have to burn. The believer must shine the light of Jesus to the world. Does this mean that the Holy Spirit, represented by air, can be used up? No, but He can be thwarted by us. We can quench the Spirit (1 Thessalonians 5:19.) Quenching occurs as a flame is deprived of air. When a believer says "no" to the Creator's will for us to do **good** things, our flame burns low and flickers.

We can also grieve the Spirit (Ephesians 4:30). Grieving the Spirit also puts out our flame because we are trying to "burn" in CO_2, which is caused by doing overt, sinful acts, and entertaining impure thoughts as part of one's way of life, while expecting to please the Creator.

From the Teacher –

A word study helps to explain the elements of this experiment:

- **hunger** (*peinao*) – be working and having no results; to crave or starve

- **filled** (*chortazo*) – to consume so much food as to gorge oneself.
- **righteousness** (*dikaiosune*) – justification by the Creator according to His standards and not ours.

This experiment is a success when the candle, or believer, has a thirst and hunger for **righteousness** which results in a burning or happy flame.

Testing the flame –

1) Does it crave time spent studying the Word of God? (yes)___ (no)___
2) Does it desire to do the good things the Spirit wills it to do? (yes)___(no)___

3) Does it no longer try to burn while entertaining a false fuel (sinning)? (yes)____ (no)____

Answer to Pop Quiz #6 – The Holy Spirit living in the believer enables or fuels the believer to do righteousness.

Homework Assignment

Observation I – A candle needs two things outside itself to do what its maker intended it to do which is to produce light. What are they?

1)_____   2)_____

Observation II – The believer needs a source of ignition, which is

3)_____

4) The believer's fuel is _____.

5) The burning light, or work of the believer is _____

_____.

Answers are found at the end of the book.

7

Producing an Act Which Meets a Need
The Merciful

One reason for conducting a lab is to test a hypothesis, which is a statement one believes to be true. The previous tests administered by the Creator in our lives have been designed to bring about changes in our souls, where the outcome may not readily be seen by others. One could say they are performed in a secret laboratory or are internally realized. We know that Jesus instructed us to pray in one's closet and to shut the door so that the Father, who sees in secret, will reward openly (Matthew 6:6).

The remaining tests are designed to test the hypothesis that Jesus has indeed changed our souls. In fact, they demonstrate publicly a transformation has occurred. This lab examines what the "failing class" of humanity considers a weakness, yet the Creator esteems of great value: **mercy**.

Pop Quiz #7 – Is the believer's attitude one that produces merciful actions?

Life Lab – *Read Matthew 5:7 and 6:14-15 – The Merciful*

Examination of the Flow of Mercy:

1) source→ 2) agent→ 3) recipient→ 4) result

1) The Creator, or *source*, acting in mercy, has forgiven the sins of the person.

2) This person has come in faith, by means of the Holy Spirit Who is the *agent* to Jesus, and has trusted in the Son's atoning work on the cross.

3) Mercy and forgiveness have gone out to that person or *recipient*.

4) The *result* is a merciful attitude and acts of mercy performed by the recipient toward others.

This is like taking a six volt battery and applying two non-insulated wire leads (*agent*) to the two terminals on top of the battery (*source*.) One lead is connected to the "+" terminal (grace) and the other to the "—" terminal (mercy). When the other end of the leads is attached to the appropriate points on a light bulb socket containing a Krypton 4.8 volt, 0.75A bulb (*recipient*), the bulb (*recipient*) burns brightly.

Take this setup to a completely dark room and repeat. The room will no longer remain dark. Others in the room will benefit from the light produced.

However, there is no guarantee others will appreciate the light, especially if they wanted to work in darkness.

Producing a Short:

Assuming that some in the room did appreciate the dark, the light can be stopped in two ways:

1) Opening the circuit or flow of energy (***mercy***) by removing one end of either wire lead from a terminal, otherwise known as a switch.

2) Creating a short circuit or short, by placing a foreign, electricity-conducting object across the non-insulated leads. This stops the light, but produces heat on the wires and the object.

From the Teacher –

The switch is controlled by the Creator. The Creator would never turn this switch off. Once the warmth and light, which are merciful acts, have been displayed, the lab has been demonstrated. The word **merciful** (*eleemon*) – meaning beneficial, meeting a need – clearly has the Creator's quality of character.

If, however, because of the ungrateful response of those who are in darkness, the recipient and displayer of mercy no longer wishes to show mercy, a short-circuit has been created. This is **not** what the Creator wants from His recipient, and the result is **heat** (*chastisement*) for the recipient.

In such cases, if the short continues, the wire leads can melt, resulting in a useless socket and bulb *(recipient)*.

Answer to Pop Quiz #7 – The source of mercy is the Creator.

Homework Assignment

1) If the set up is performed according to instructions the result is _____ and _____.

2) If the set up is shorted, the result is _____ and _____.

Answers are found at the end of the book.

-8-

The Pop Quiz for the Control Center
Purity of Heart

"For as he thinketh in his heart, so is he…" (Proverbs 23:7)

"Keep thy heart with all diligence; for out of it are the lessons of life." (Proverbs 4:23)

S o often circumstances arise in our daily lives that show us, upon reflection, who we really are. These incidents are ordered by the Creator. We are in His laboratory. The heart or will is the control center of a human being. How we react is based on our relationship with Him, and flows out of our control center. Is your relationship in good repair? Do you *have* a relationship with Him through His Son?

Pop Quiz #8 – How does a child of the Creator know he has a pure heart?

Life Lab – *Read Matthew 5:8 – The Pure in Heart*

You most likely will not be able to actually perform this lab because of the expensive equipment and a costly substance: *gold*.

When gold is mined, it often is not the brightly shining metal one would see in a refined bar or coin. Depending on where it was mined, it even has hues, such as the pinkish cast in the gold from South Africa.

You will need:

- A sample of raw, mined gold ore (1 troy oz. or more)
- A small, steel shell, coreless furnace (or a channel, crucible, or direct electric heat furnace), with a maximum operating temperature of 1400 degrees Celsius, and a maximum continuous operating temperature of 1350 degrees Celsius.

When gold is smelted in an extremely hot crucible, the impurities rise to the surface, where they are either skimmed off or removed by some other process. The result is a mirror-like surface. In the ancient world, the refiner knew he had a pure product when he could see his face reflected back from the surface of the gold.

Thus, God will, "purge them as gold and silver that they may offer unto the Lord an offering in righteousness" (Malachi 3:3). Job said, "...when He hath tried me, I shall come forth as gold" (Job 23:10).

From the Teacher –

The word pure, (*katharos*) meaning to make pure by cleansing from contaminants, is used when describing the purification of precious metals such as gold. It is closely related to the Latin word for chaste. In psychology it portrays an emptying of destructive emotions. In Romans 7:15-25, Paul dealt with the conflict he felt between purity and the defilement of his flesh.

The pop quizzes God conducts us through, or tries us in, produce the awareness that we need a pure heart. A solid prayer life, coupled with personal Bible study and living daily under the control and filling of the Holy Spirit will produce and maintain a pure heart.

When God sees His image, His ways and His character, reflected in our lives, He knows that our hearts are pure.

Answer to Pop Quiz #8 – It is pure when the child *sees* God reflected there.

Homework Assignment

What does the answer to Pop Quiz 8 listed above mean?

1) _____

2) _____

3) _____

Answers are found at the end of the book.

Not an Absence,
but a Presence
The Peacemakers

We live in a world that is at war. Peace is spoken of, but is of a greater rarity than gold. History tells us that every "peace" treaty ever signed has one singularity: **All** have been broken.

When asked to describe peace, this substance is often described by one or more things that are absent: war, hate, rioting, bitterness, divided loyalties, and the like. But is that the kind of peace which the Creator offers? No, there is a much deeper and more satisfying peace that only His children know or can know. It is the presence of the Prince of Peace in the pure heart of one of His own.

The connection between these blessings from the Creator can be seen in James 3:17-18, "But the wisdom that is from above is first pure, then peaceable... And the fruit of righteousness is sown in peace of them that make peace."

Pop Quiz #9 – How does righteousness make one a peacemaker?

Life Lab – *Read Matthew 5:9 – The Peacemakers*

You have probably heard of pouring oil on troubled waters. This refers to a person attempting to bring peace to a troubled situation. When waters are "stirred up" or wash back and forth as in a large kettle, the water will splash over the sides and out of the container. When the surface of the water is covered with oil which is the same temperature as the water, it floats on top of the "troubled waters," thus containing the water.

It is interesting that oil is symbolic of the Holy Spirit in Scripture. Since the believer is sealed with the Holy Spirit (Ephesians 1:13) and is commanded to be filled with Him (Ephesians 5:18), the believer has the capability of being a peacemaker.

But combining oil with water does not always produce so peaceable an outcome. If oil is heated and water is thrown on it – (do

not try this!) – an explosion **will** follow – with burning oil scattered everywhere.

A variation of this often happened to the Apostle Paul when he brought the gospel to various towns where the powerful did not want to hear it – the town exploded when they tried to douse the gospel with their "cold water." It was neither Paul nor his fellow workers who did the exploding.

From the Teacher –

As the following terms are essential to the outcome of this lab, a brief study of these words follows:

peacemaker (*eirenopoios*) – one who makes peace, quietness, rest, calm

righteousness (*dikaiosune*) – fairness or rightness of character, actions

Of course the question is, "How can sinful creatures be declared right in character?" The answer is more "who" than "how." The one who has not received Christ is in inward turmoil. He or she has no peace. There is one remedy: "Therefore being justified by faith, we have **peace with** God through our Lord Jesus Christ" (Romans 5:1, 10:10). We have been justified by faith and the **peace of** God is now ours. We have, as it were, put on the righteousness of Christ (Romans 10:4, Revelation 19:8).

Since the believer has peace within and without, he is now an ambassador of Christ (2 Corinthians 5:20) and therefore brings peace to **individuals** in turmoil. The world, the ones with the "failing gene" (Chapter One, Fact Four), do not like having their failure talked about, so peace may be the last thing some people will want to experience when shown the Savior.

Answer to Pop Quiz #9 – We are the Creator's children because we are like His only begotten Son, the Prince of Peace.

Homework Assignment

1) Did Jesus understand the explosive nature of the gospel?_____

2) Where can this be found? _____

Answers are found at the end of the book.

The Crucible
The Persecuted for Righteousness' Sake

I t should be noted that many "experiments" create heat as a byproduct. As a point in fact, the reason our bodies have a temperature is that the chemical processes taking place within us which are part of physical life produce heat. But some labs require heat to be applied to the elements in order that the desired result can occur. In some cases, the substances are combined in a ceramic vessel called a crucible. It creates a space where forces of heat are concentrated to change the combined elements into a new substance. The root of the word crucible is "cross."

"Blessed are they which are persecuted for righteousness' sake: for theirs is the kingdom of heaven. Blessed are ye, when men shall revile you, and persecute you, and shall say all manner of evil against you **falsely,** for *My* sake. Rejoice, and be exceeding glad: for great is your reward in heaven: for so persecuted they the prophets which were before you." (Matthew 5:10-12 emphasis added)

In all previous tests or labs, the Creator pronounced us blessed or "happy." While the early labs (Chapters 3-6) were designed for our own internal change and awareness, the last three labs (Chapters 7 – 9) were to be viewed by all as they conform us to the image of the Creator Himself (Romans 8:29, 12:2).

As our Creator is now presenting the summation of all our pop quizzes and labs, I suppose you could call this the "final exam." Some people are terrified of finals. I remember in my college days, there were some courses in my major field that had only two exams. One course had as the only grade a lengthy research paper. After some time, I learned that keeping on top of each lab, each assignment, and every test no matter the size, would result in being "ready" for the final exam. Certainly I still had to prepare, but I now knew the direction this final would take.

That is what Jesus has been saying in the beatitudes. And that is what He has been doing in your life and mine. We live in times which were forecast long ago. The "heat" is being turned up. The adversary knows the day is fast approaching when his time will become short (Revelation 12:12).

We have "good news" that our Advocate (1 John 2:1) promised never to leave us, nor forsake us (John 14:18, 2 Corinthians 4:9). Speaking of heat, He was with the children of Israel in the desert wanderings with Moses (1 Corinthians 10:4).

He was also with Hananiah ("Jehovah is gracious"), Mishael ("Who is *what* God is"), and Azariah ("Jehovah has helped"). You probably know them by their Babylonian names; Shadrach, Meshach and Abednego. In Daniel chapter three, they refused to bow and worship the image Nebuchadnezzar set up. In his fury, the king tells them, "...who is God that shall deliver you out of my hands?"

They replied, "O Nebuchadnezzar, we are not careful to answer thee in this matter. If it be so, our God, whom we serve is able to deliver us from the burning fiery furnace, and He will deliver us out of thine hand, O king. *But if not*, be it known unto thee, O king, that we will not serve thy gods, nor worship the golden image which thou hast set up" (Daniel 3:16-18).

Once they are thrown into the furnace, the king says, "Lo, I see four men loose, walking in the midst of the fire, and they have no hurt; and the fourth is like the Son of God" (Daniel 3:25). This same Creator is the Son of God. He is able to deliver us. But He may choose **instead** to go with us through the crucible. He may deliver us out of it, or call us home. But He will always be with us. Pass the test – by trusting in Him to the uttermost.

There is so much more to be found in Christ's teachings. In fact, the Bible is a treasure trove waiting to be discovered by you, His child. The hunger you sense for more insight into these topics comes from the Creator's Spirit within you. As a new Christian, you need "the sincere milk of the word, that you may grow thereby" (1 Peter 2:2).

For those who are older in the Lord, meat is your desire (1 Corinthians 3:2). This book has given you an appetite for "bulking up" your spiritual constitution. Develop the habits of the Bereans, who "received the word with all readiness of mind, and searched the Scripture daily, whether those things were so" (Acts 17:10-11).

Oh, by the way, where you were looking for the **prizes** I mentioned earlier?

Well, here is your treasure map to find them for yourself:

James 1:12 _____

2 Timothy 4:8 _____

1 Peter 5:4 _____

1 Corinthians 9:25 _____

1 Thessalonians 2:19 _____

Now, go and search for the buried treasure in each scripture.

Answers for Chapter Quizzes

Chapter 3:

1. C	4. Pharisee	7. genuine humility
2. A	5. tax-gatherer	8. gaining the kingdom of heaven
3. B	6. tax-gatherer	

Chapter 5:

1) Joseph did not retaliate against his brothers for selling him into slavery.

2) Jesus could have called thousands of angels to defend Him. He did not need Peter (or us) to defend Him.

Chapter 6:

1) a spark

2) a source of fuel (air)

3) the Creator

4) the Holy Spirit

5) testimony or telling others of the Creator's free gift to them

Chapter 7:

1) light (insight, revelation) and warmth (on a heart cold toward the Creator)

2) darkness (no gospel going forth) and heat (correction for the believer)

Chapter 8:

1) We begin to live in God's presence (ignorance of God obscures Him).

2) We see God working in and around us (ministering to others rids us of selfishness).

3) Job 42:5, "I have heard Thee by the hearing of the ear; but now my eye sees Thee."

Chapter 9:

1) yes

2) **John 14:27,** "Peace I leave with you, my peace I give unto you: not as the world giveth, give I unto you. Let not your heart be troubled, neither let it be afraid."

Luke 12:51, "Suppose ye that I am come to give peace on earth? I tell you, Nay; but rather division."